CHARLOTTE E. RAY:

TRAILBLAZING LAWYER

NANCY LOEWEN

Text Copyright © 2025 Planting People Growing Justice Press
Illustrations copyright © 2025 Planting People Growing Justice Press

Cover Artwork and Illustrations by Whimsical Designs by CJ
Design by Reyhana Ismail

All rights reserved.

No part of this book may be reproduced in any manner without express written consent of the publisher, except in the case of brief excerpts in critical reviews and articles.

All inquiries or sales request should be addressed to:

Planting People Growing Justice Press
P.O. Box 131894
Saint Paul, MN 55113
www.ppgjli.org

Printed and bound in the United States of America
First Edition
LCCN: 2024951705
1-9781959223641/9798896050001-04/15/2025

DEDICATION

This book is dedicated to For Veronica (Ronnie) Burton, educator and changemaker

TABLE OF CONTENTS

Introduction
Breaking Barriers 4

Chapter 1:
A Change-Making Family 6

Chapter 2:
Eager to Learn 11

Chapter 3:
First Female Lawyer 17

Chapter 4:
Widening the Path 20

About the Author 25

Ways to Make a Difference 26

Glossary 28

Books, Websites, Source Notes 30

Words in **bold** are in the glossary.

BREAKING BARRIERS

In 1872, at the age of 22, Charlotte E. Ray made history. She broke many barriers to become the first Black female lawyer in the United States.

This was a truly remarkable feat. At that time, most women did not have jobs. Those who did were likely to be nurses or maids. Women did not have the right to an education. They could not even vote.

Black people faced additional injustices. In 1865, the Civil War had brought an end to slavery, but the nation was far from peaceful. Racism and violence were widespread. Black people were constantly struggling with unfair laws, business practices, and social customs.

Despite these challenges, Charlotte Ray refused to let her gender or race hold her back. She pressed forward and achieved her dream of becoming both a teacher and a lawyer. Her determination and success paved the way for future leaders.

CHAPTER 1:
A CHANGE-MAKING FAMILY

Charlotte Ray was born to Charles Bennet Ray and Charlotte Augusta Burroughs on January 13, 1850. She was one of seven children. The family lived in New York City, where Charles was a pastor, writer, and editor. He was a noted leader in the Black community.

The Rays cared deeply about ending slavery and changing unfair laws. They were active in the Underground Railroad, opening their home to Black people escaping slavery. From the time she was a young girl, Charlotte heard the stories of people who took great risks in order to be free.

On January 1, 1863, when Charlotte was nearly thirteen years old, President Abraham Lincoln signed the Emancipation Proclamation. This law gave all enslaved people their freedom. It was an enormous triumph—the first step toward equality.

HIDDEN PATHS TO FREEDOM

The Underground Railroad helped thousands of **enslaved** Black people get to the North or Canada, where they could be free. Brave, caring people (both Black and white) secretly opened up their homes and provided food and shelter. They planned routes so travelers could go from one safe house to the next. The Underground Railroad operated between the late 1700s and the end of the Civil War in 1865.

The nation was in the middle of the Civil War, however, and would remain in turmoil for years to come. In fact, later that year, New York City experienced the worst riots in U.S. history. A new law required men of certain ages to sign up for the military. Their names would be put into a lottery. If their name was selected, they would have to fight. But if men could afford to pay a fee or hire someone to take their place, they did not have to go to war. Black men were not included in this law. They were not considered citizens.

Many poor white immigrants were furious that the law favored the rich. And they were furious with Black people. They blamed Black people for the war and were scared that Black men from the South would take their jobs. Horrible riots broke out on July 13 and lasted for days. Hundreds of people died. Many Black families lost all that they owned. It took 4,000 federal troops to stop the violence.

For months, Charlotte Ray's father worked with businesses and other ministers to help families affected by the riots. She saw firsthand how courage and compassion could make a community stronger.

NORTH AGAINST SOUTH

The American Civil War (1861–1865) pitted the Northern states (Union) against the Southern states (Confederacy). Confederates believed that states should be able to make their own decisions about slavery. They threatened to withdraw from the Union. Unionists wanted to keep the nation together. They wanted to end the practice of slavery. More than half a million people died in the war. The Union won, but the effects of the war are still felt today.

CHAPTER 2:
EAGER TO LEARN

The Ray family believed that education was important for both boys and girls. Charlotte Ray attended the Institute for the Education of Colored Youth in Washington, D.C. This school had been started by a white woman named Myrtilla Miner. Earlier in her career, Miner had not been allowed to teach Black girls. She did not think that was right, so she decided to open her own school. Many of Miner's students went on to teach. Some even opened schools of their own.

After finishing school in 1869, Ray stayed in Washington, D.C. She trained other teachers at Howard Preparatory School. But Ray had another goal. She wanted to become a lawyer.

This was a brave dream. No woman, Black or white, was a practicing lawyer at that time. Women had not been allowed into the profession. Most law schools did not accept women. And most states did not allow women to take the bar exam. (The bar exam is a long, hard test that people must pass in order to practice law.)

Times were changing, however. In 1869, a white woman named Arabella Mansfield passed the Iowa bar exam. She had not gone to law school. Instead, she had studied at her brother's law office. But Mansfield never practiced law. She became a college English professor instead.

Ada H. Kepley, also white, graduated from a Chicago law school in 1870. She may have been the first woman in the world to graduate from law school. But she never practiced law, either. She was not allowed to take the Illinois bar exam. Her husband was a lawyer, and together they challenged the Illinois law. They won, and women were allowed to take the bar exam in Illinois beginning in 1872. But by that time, Kepley was deeply involved in other social reform work. She never took the bar exam.

Like Mansfield and Kepley, Charlotte Ray was not going to let old rules keep her from breaking new ground. Howard University Law School accepted women as students, so Ray enrolled. She taught during the day and took law classes in the evenings. She was known as a careful, thoughtful student.

AN IMPORTANT HBCU (HISTORICALLY BLACK COLLEGES AND UNIVERSITIES)

Howard University opened in 1867 in Washington, D.C. Its goal was to provide educational opportunities for Black people after the Civil War. Today it is one of the top schools in the nation.

Ray graduated from law school on February 27, 1872. Frederick Douglass, an important Black leader, wrote about Ray in his weekly newspaper.

> *The first colored lady in the world to graduate in law graduated from Howard University on this occasion. Her essay on "Chancery" was well received, and her bravery and* **perseverance** *highly appreciated. Miss Charlotte E. Ray, the graduate, is the daughter of the Rev. Charles B. Ray, of New York, well and favorably known in that city.*

The next step was passing the District of Columbia bar exam. It's possible that Ray hid the fact that she was woman. She may have written her initials on the application instead of her full name. We may never know for sure. What we do know is that she was admitted to the bar of the District of Columbia on April 23, 1872.

As a Black woman, Charlotte Ray had graduated from law school and been admitted to the bar. She had truly made history.

ANOTHER TRAILBLAZER

Mary Ann Shadd Cary was the first Black female newspaper editor in North America. She also earned a law degree from Howard University eleven years after Ray. Shadd Cary was born in Delaware in 1823. Her family was active in the Underground Railroad. When Congress passed a law making it illegal to help enslaved people, she moved to Canada with her brother. There she published an antislavery newspaper. She returned to the United States to help the Union effort at the start of the Civil War. She was an **activist**, teacher, and writer the rest of her life.

CHAPTER 3:
FIRST FEMALE LAWYER

Ray opened her law practice in Washington, D.C., in 1872. She wanted to work with businesses. However, the only case that Ray worked on that we know of today had to do with a divorce. Martha Gadley was a Black woman whose husband became very violent when he drank. Gadley wanted a divorce, but the court didn't allow it. Gadley decided to **appeal**, and Charlotte Ray agreed to help.

Ray argued Gadley's case before the District of Columbia Supreme Court—and won. It was a stunning victory at a time when women didn't have many rights.

Ray's success in the Gadley case did not help her law practice, however. People were not ready to trust a Black woman with their legal concerns. She had no choice but to close her practice. In 1879, she returned to New York City.

ODE TO LINCOLN

Charlotte's sister, Henrietta Cordelia Ray, was a poet. Her poem "Lincoln" was read at the **dedication** of the **Emancipation Memorial** in Washington, D.C., in April 1876. President Ulysses S. Grant attended the ceremony. Frederick Douglass gave a speech.

While Ray's career as a lawyer was over, she was still helping others. She taught in Brooklyn's public school system for many years. She worked to gain voting rights for women. She was also among the earliest members of the National Association of Colored Women.

Little else is known about Ray's life. She married a man named Fraim in the late 1880s. In 1897, she moved to Woodside, Queens (New York). She died on January 4, 1911, most likely from bronchitis. She was 60 years old.

Although much of Ray's life remains a mystery, she will never be forgotten. She broke barriers that needed to be broken. Gradually, more law schools began admitting women. More states allowed women to take the bar exam. By the late 1800s and early 1900s, many more women were entering the legal profession thanks to trailblazers like Charlotte Ray.

CHAPTER 4:
WIDENING THE PATH

Over the years and across the country, Black women have continued to make history. Here are just a few examples of the many Black women who have transformed the field of law.

Jane Matilda Bolin (1908 - 2007) was the first Black female judge. She was appointed to New York City's family court in 1939 at the age of 31. She served for forty years. And that wasn't her only "first." Bolin was the first Black woman to graduate from Yale Law School. She was also the first Black woman to join the New York City Bar.

In 1966, Constance Baker Motley (1921 - 2005) became the first Black female federal judge. She was appointed by President Lyndon B. Johnson and served the Southern District of New York. Throughout her career, she fought hard for **civil rights**. She played a key role in the 1954 landmark Supreme Court decision that ended school **segregation**.

Paulette Brown (b. 1951) was the first Black woman to be president of the American Bar Association (ABA). The ABA is an influential organization of people who work in the field of law. Its goal is to improve the justice system. Paulette Brown served as ABA president from 2015 to 2016. In her leadership, she called attention to the value of **diversity**.

Loretta E. Lynch (b. 1959) was the first Black female attorney general. She was appointed by President Barack Obama in 2015 and served for two years. The attorney general is the head of the U.S. Department of Justice. This person in this role gives advice to the President and other members of the Executive Branch.

Until recently, there had never been a U.S. vice president who was not white and male. As a Black Asian woman, Kamala Harris (b. 1964) changed that story. She became vice president following the election of President Joe Biden in 2020. Kamala Harris was also the first woman of color to serve California as attorney general and senator.

In 2022, Ketanji Brown Jackson (b. 1970) became the first Black woman to serve as a Supreme Court justice. She was appointed by President Joe Biden. The Supreme Court is the highest court of the land. Its nine justices make important decisions about our country's laws.

These accomplished women and countless others have been inspired by Charlotte Ray. Ray believed in her own abilities. She believed in her right to a good education. She believed in her right to pursue her dreams—even if it meant challenging expectations. Charlotte Ray opened a door that will never be closed.

ABOUT THE AUTHOR

Nancy Loewen grew up on a farm in southwestern Minnesota, surrounded by library books and cats.

She's published more than 140 books for children and young adults, including *The Everybody Club, Writer's Toolbox*, and *The LAST Day of Kindergarten* (a Minnesota Book Award finalist).

She lives in St. Paul.

WAYS TO MAKE A DIFFERENCE

TRY HARD AT SCHOOL.
Make the most of the opportunities that come your way. Charlotte Ray and her family believed that education was the key to a better life. We owe it to ourselves to learn, grow, and develop our talents.

HELP OTHERS LEARN, TOO.
Share what you know and be willing to work together with others. Ray and her sisters were teachers most of their lives. They cared about their students and their communities.

BE WILLING TO STAND OUT.
It must have been hard for Charlotte Ray to be the only woman in her law classes, but she did it anyway. She knew she belonged there, even if not everyone agreed.

CHALLENGE UNFAIR SYSTEMS.
Ray gave her all to the case of Martha Gadley. At that time, few people cared about a Black woman's right to leave an abusive marriage. But Ray was different. She

stood up for what was right and convinced others to do so as well.

DON'T GIVE IN TO "ALL OR NOTHING" THINKING.

After all her hard work, Ray ended up not being able make a living as a lawyer. She must have been discouraged, but she didn't give up. She knew she could make a difference by teaching and working for women's rights.

GLOSSARY

Activist	A person who works hard to bring about change
Bronchitis	A disease of the lungs that makes it difficult to breathe
Civil rights (or rights)	The rights given by a government to its people. Examples include the right to vote, the right to a fair trial, the right to a public education, and the right to practice one's religion
Dedication	A service or program that celebrates the opening of something new, such as a building or park
Diversity	Including people with many backgrounds
Emancipation	the process of being set free
Enslaved	to be forced by another person into a position of slavery. Enslaved people were not allowed civil rights and were made to do whatever the enslavers demanded

Memorial	something that honors an important event or a person who has died
Perseverence	to work steadily toward a goal
Segregation	a system in which people are separated from each other based on race or other factors

BOOKS

Anderson, Kirsten, and Manuel Gutiérrez. (2021). *Who is Kamala Harris?* Penguin Workshop.

Hudson, Cheryl Willis. (2020). *Brave. Black. First.: 50+ African American Women Who Changed the World.* Crown Books for Young Readers.

Schwartz, Heather E. (2023). *Ketanji Brown Jackson: First Black Woman on the US Supreme Court.* Lerner Publications.

WEBSITES

Britannica
Charlotte E. Ray
American lawyer and teacher
britannica.com/biography/Charlotte-E-Ray

Kiddle
Charlotte E. Ray facts for kids
kids.kiddle.co/Charlotte_E._Ray

History.com
Charlotte E. Ray's Brief But Historic Career as the First U.S. Black Woman Attorney
history.com/news/charlotte-e-ray-first-black-woman-attorney

SOURCE NOTES

Ashar, Dr. Linda C. "Gadley vs. Gadley Archives." *APU Edge.* apuedge.com/tag/gadley-vs-gadley/.

Blakemore, Erin. "Charlotte E. Ray's Brief but Historic Career as the First U.S. Black Woman Attorney." History.com. history.com/news/charlotte-e-ray-first-black-woman-attorney.

"Full Text of 'Sketch of the Life of Rev. Charles B. Ray.'" Internet Archive. https://archive.org/stream/9342f943-b613-491a-9d22-1f733a906f7c/9342f943-b613-491a-9d22-1f733a906f7c_djvu.txt.

New National Era. (Washington, DC), 1900-02-29. loc.gov/item/sn84026753/1872-02-29/ed-1/.

Smith, J. Clay Jr. "Charlotte E. Ray Pleads before Court." Howard Law Journal, vol. 43, no. 2, Winter 2000, pp. 121-140. HeinOnline.

ABOUT PLANTING PEOPLE GROWING JUSTICE LEADERSHIP INSTITUTE

Planting People Growing Justice Leadership Institute seeks to plant seeds of social change through education, training, and community outreach.

A portion of the proceeds from this book will support the educational programming of Planting People Growing Justice Leadership Institute.